HOW IT WORKS

Electric Guitars

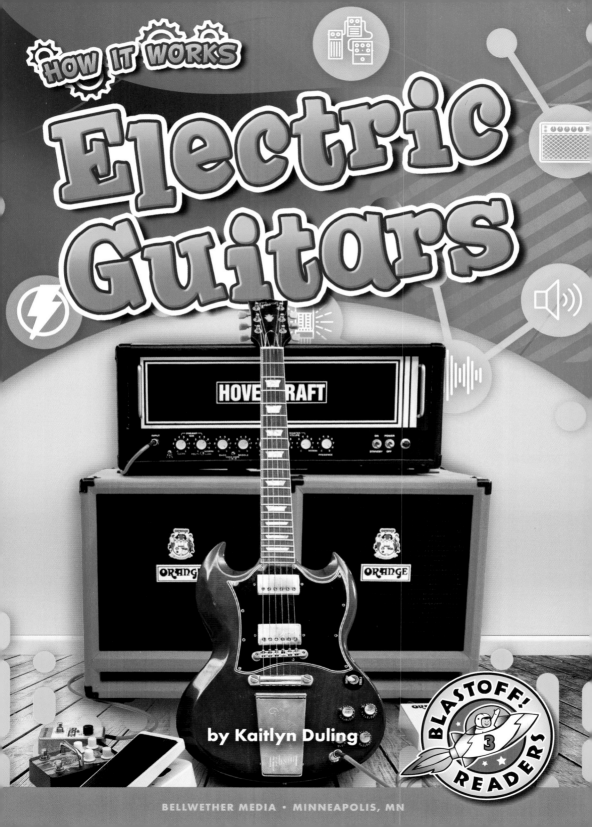

HOVERCRAFT

ORANGE

ORANGE

by Kaitlyn Duling

BLASTOFF! READERS 3

BELLWETHER MEDIA • MINNEAPOLIS, MN

Blastoff! Readers are carefully developed by literacy experts to build reading stamina and move students toward fluency by combining standards-based content with developmentally appropriate text.

Level 1 provides the most support through repetition of high-frequency words, light text, predictable sentence patterns, and strong visual support.

Level 2 offers early readers a bit more challenge through varied sentences, increased text load, and text-supportive special features.

Level 3 advances early-fluent readers toward fluency through increased text load, less reliance on photos, advancing concepts, longer sentences, and more complex special features.

★ **Blastoff! Universe**

Reading Level

Grade **K**

Grades **1–3**

Grade **4**

This edition first published in 2023 by Bellwether Media, Inc.

No part of this publication may be reproduced in whole or in part without written permission of the publisher. For information regarding permission, write to Bellwether Media, Inc., Attention: Permissions Department, 6012 Blue Circle Drive, Minnetonka, MN 55343.

Library of Congress Cataloging-in-Publication Data

Names: Duling, Kaitlyn, author.
Title: Electric guitars / by Kaitlyn Duling.
Description: Minneapolis : Bellwether Media, 2023. | Series: How it works | Includes bibliographical references and index. | Audience: Ages 5-8 | Audience: Grades 2-3 | Summary: "Simple text and full-color photography introduce beginning readers to electric guitars. Developed by literacy experts for students in kindergarten through third grade" -- Provided by publisher.
Identifiers: LCCN 2022020063 (print) | LCCN 2022020064 (ebook) | ISBN 9781644877333 (library binding) | ISBN 9781648347795 (ebook)
Subjects: LCSH: Electric guitar--Juvenile literature.
Classification: LCC ML1015.G9 D94 2023 (print) | LCC ML1015.G9 (ebook) | DDC 787.87/192--dc23/eng/20220422
LC record available at https://lccn.loc.gov/2022020063
LC ebook record available at https://lccn.loc.gov/2022020064

Editor: Rachael Barnes   Series Design: Jeffrey Kollock   Book Designer: Josh Brink

Printed in the United States of America, North Mankato, MN.

Table of Contents

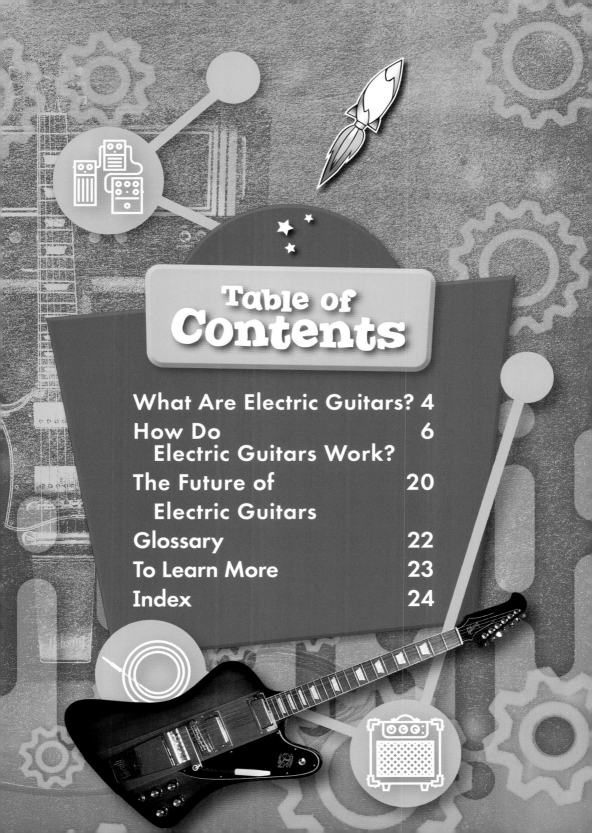

What Are Electric Guitars?

Electric guitars are musical instruments. They are used to play different types of music.

Blues and jazz use electric guitars. Country, pop, and rock do, too!

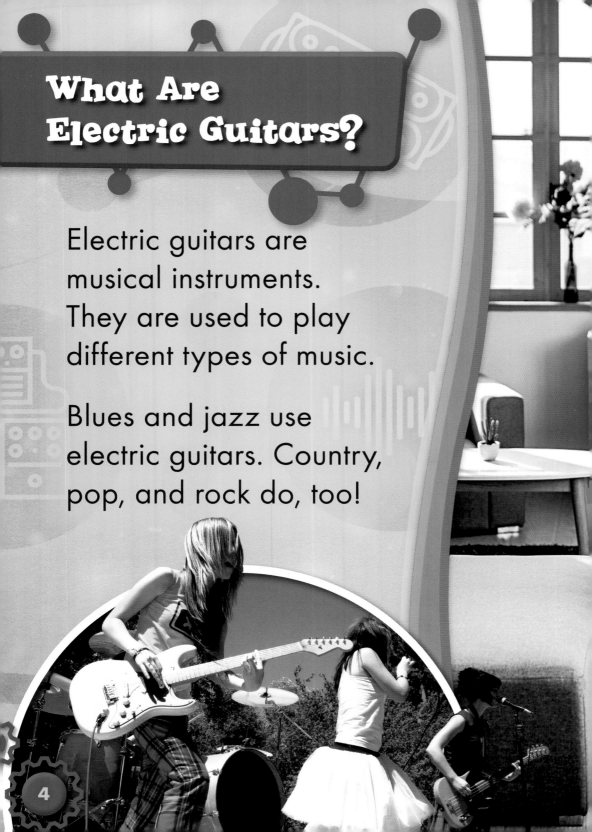

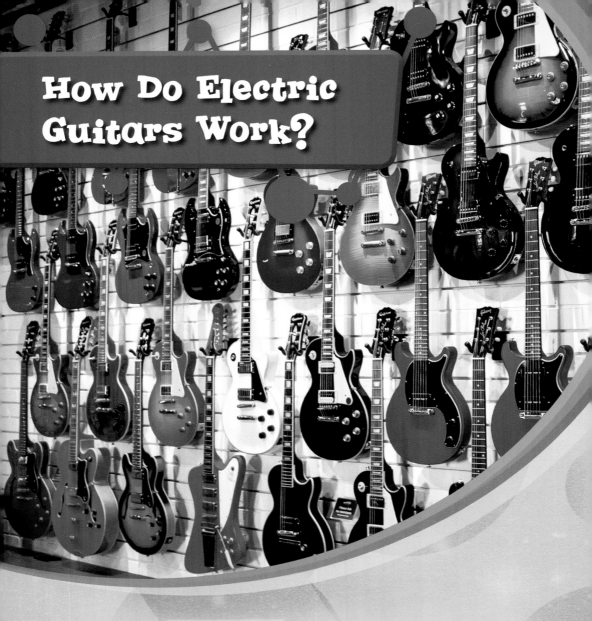

How Do Electric Guitars Work?

There are many styles of electric guitar. Their bodies are often made of wood. Different types of wood produce different sounds.

Most guitars are coated in **resin** or painted. This keeps the wood safe.

electric guitar with resin coating

pick

Electric guitars have six or more metal strings. Players **strum** or pluck the strings. Sometimes they use a **pick**.

Players can make many different sounds!

Parts of an Electric Guitar

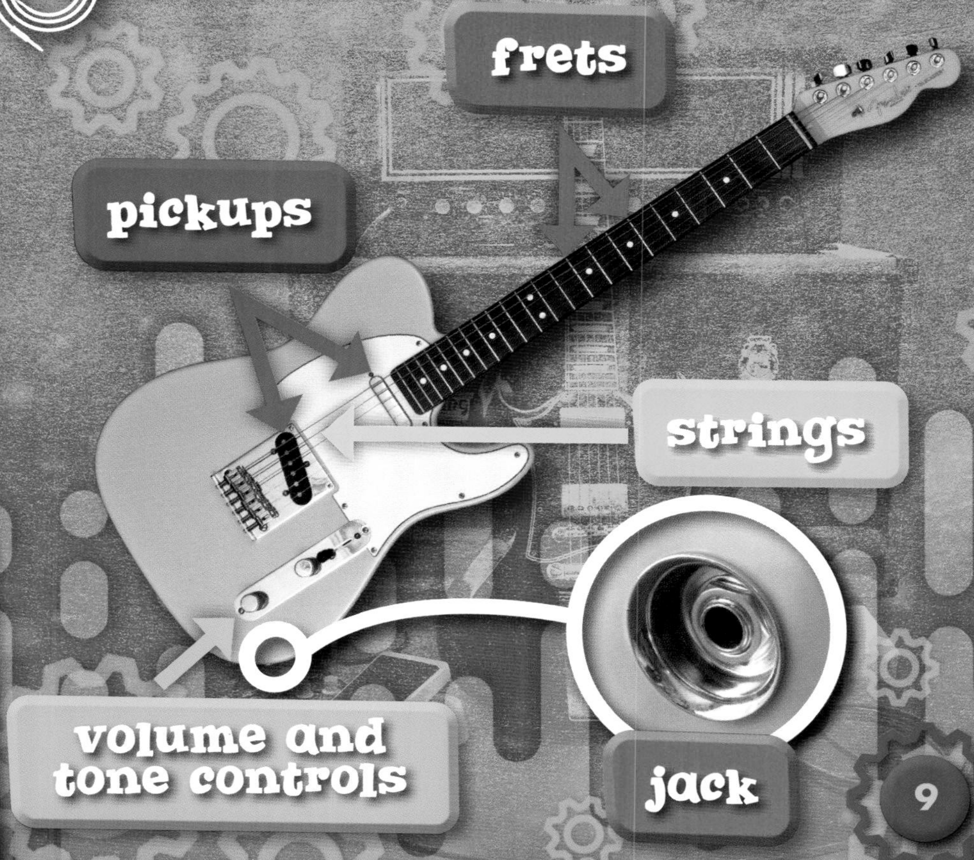

frets

pickups

strings

volume and tone controls

jack

9

To play a note, players pluck a string. It **vibrates** and makes a sound.

plucking

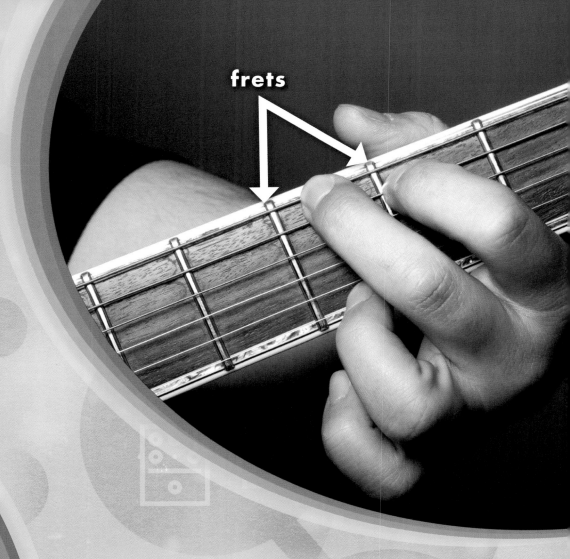

frets

Pressing down on a string changes how it vibrates. Metal lines called frets show players where to press. Players make new notes!

pickups

Electric guitar strings vibrate above devices called **pickups**. A pickup has a set of **magnets** and a **coil** of wire.

Electric Guitar Pickup

guitar
string

magnet

coil of wire

magnetic
field

The coil circles the magnets.
This creates a **magnetic field**
between the strings and the pickup.

When strummed, the vibrating strings move the magnetic field. This creates an **electric current**.

This current carries the sound of each moving string.

volume and tone controls

VOLUME

The electric current moves around the coil in the pickup. It passes through the guitar's **volume** and **tone** controls.

It leaves the guitar through
a **jack** connected to a cable.

jack

cable

17

ker

The electric current travels
through the cable to an **amp**.
The amp changes the electric
current into sound.

Finally, the sound goes to a speaker. The notes the player strummed come out!

How Electric Current Travels

amp

speakers

electric current

The Future of Electric Guitars

Electric guitars use magnets. But some guitars are going **digital**. They can connect to **smartphones**.

No matter what, electric guitars are always going to rock!

Question

If you were a guitar player,
what type of music
would you play?

21

Glossary

amp—an electronic device that makes sounds louder; amp is short for amplifier.

coil—a length of something wrapped in circles around something else; an electric guitar coil is a thin, long wire that wraps around the magnets in a pickup.

digital—related to electronics or computers

electric current—an electric charge in motion

jack—an opening for a cable that connects the guitar to an amp

magnetic field—the area around a magnet that is affected by its force

magnets—pieces of metal that pull other metals towards them

pick—a small object used to strum or pluck guitar strings

pickups—devices that convert electric guitar string vibrations into an electric current

resin—a substance that dries clear and is often used to keep surfaces safe from harm

smartphones—cell phones with advanced features such as internet access and apps

strum—to sweep a finger or pick across guitar strings

tone—a musical sound of a certain kind

vibrates—moves rapidly back and forth

volume—how loud or quiet something sounds

To Learn More

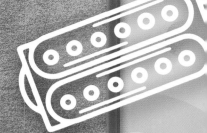

AT THE LIBRARY

Amin, Anita Nahta. *Electricity*. Minneapolis, Minn.: Jump!, 2022.

Morland, Charlie. *Music and How it Works*. New York, N.Y.: DK Children, 2020.

Tomsic, Kim. *Guitar Genius: How Les Paul Engineered the Solid-Body Electric Guitar and Rocked the World*. San Francisco, Calif.: Chronicle Books, 2019.

ON THE WEB

FACTSURFER

Factsurfer.com gives you a safe, fun way to find more information.

1. Go to www.factsurfer.com.

2. Enter "electric guitars" into the search box and click 🔍.

3. Select your book cover to see a list of related content.

Index

The images in this book are reproduced through the courtesy of: Josh Brink, cover (hero), p. 3; The_Molostock, cover (background); Photobank.kiev.ua, p. 4 (band); South_agency, pp. 4-5; Solarisys, p. 6; Bozidar Acimov, p. 7; Wachiwit, p. 8; dean bertoncelj, p. 9; kittayot kunjuntarachot, p. 9 (jack); Dmitriy_Tsyupa, p. 10; Stocked House Studio, p. 11; Christopher Tipton, pp. 12-13; Jay-Dee, p. 14; Ron Sumners/ Alamy Stock Photo, p. 15; Drpixel, p. 16; Boris Bulychev, p. 17; BristolMusic, p. 18; Arief Pritono/ Getty Images, p. 20; Robert Niedring/ Alamy Stock Photo, pp. 20-21 (guitarist); malinar, pp. 20-21 (marshall amp); U.P.images_photo, p. 23.